Our Future

How Kids are Taking Action

written and illustrated by Janet Wilson

Second Story Press

To my dear friend, Linda Sword,
humble champion of many worthy causes.
And to Grandmother Water Walker, Josephine Mandamin,
who taught us that water is life.

"One mosquito can't do anything against a rhino, but a thousand mosquitoes together can make a rhino change its direction."

—Felix Finkbeiner, Plant for the Planet

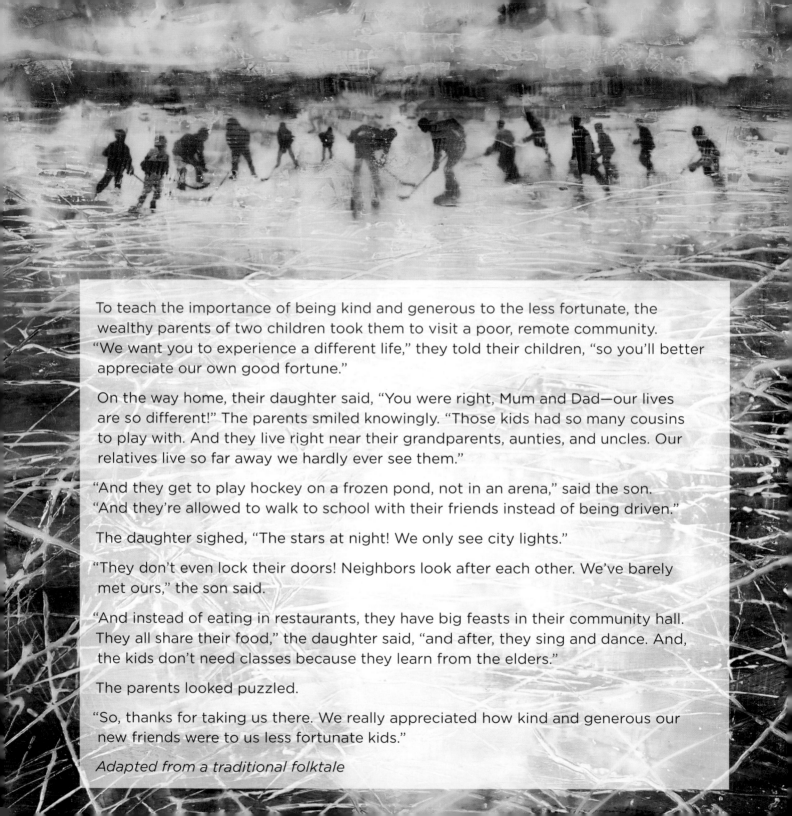

To teach the importance of being kind and generous to the less fortunate, the wealthy parents of two children took them to visit a poor, remote community. "We want you to experience a different life," they told their children, "so you'll better appreciate our own good fortune."

On the way home, their daughter said, "You were right, Mum and Dad—our lives are so different!" The parents smiled knowingly. "Those kids had so many cousins to play with. And they live right near their grandparents, aunties, and uncles. Our relatives live so far away we hardly ever see them."

"And they get to play hockey on a frozen pond, not in an arena," said the son. "And they're allowed to walk to school with their friends instead of being driven."

The daughter sighed, "The stars at night! We only see city lights."

"They don't even lock their doors! Neighbors look after each other. We've barely met ours," the son said.

"And instead of eating in restaurants, they have big feasts in their community hall. They all share their food," the daughter said, "and after, they sing and dance. And, the kids don't need classes because they learn from the elders."

The parents looked puzzled.

"So, thanks for taking us there. We really appreciated how kind and generous our new friends were to us less fortunate kids."

Adapted from a traditional folktale

"The world is ruled by adults, but it will be the children who inherit the consequences of today's decisions...good and bad. So we stand here before you advocating for our future."
—**Franny Ladell Yakelashek** and **Rupert Yakelashek**, Canadian environmental activists.

As anyone will admit, listening to the news can be scary—hurricanes, school shootings, forest fires, wars. What are we to make of a world that seems ever more troubled and fragile? Though grown-ups say, "Don't worry, children. We'll take care of the world's problems," they have a track record of making short-sighted decisions that do not "take care" of kids' lives and futures at all. As Felix Finkbeiner, a young German activist says, "If you let a monkey choose if he wants one banana now or six bananas later, the monkey will always choose the one banana now. We children understood we cannot trust that adults alone will save our future...we have to take our future in our own hands."

And so kids are taking action—rising to question the sanity of common practices. Their strengths are passion, imagination, and hope. And with these powerful strengths, they are reminding grown-ups of what is most important: to love family and friends above money; to share and treat others equally; to take care of our only planet. Felix advises, "Do not wait for adults to act. Together, we want to show that everyone can do something for our future and that together, as a world family, we can solve these problems."
—Janet Wilson

All of us have some activist in us. Maybe you witnessed an injustice and couldn't forget it—you just *had* to do something. Kids who become activists take positive action because they feel they have no choice: they *have* to learn more about an issue, raise awareness, and bring about change.

"Young people are a part of the largest generation in history—two billion strong. Around the globe, young people are coming together to build a movement for success.... Yes, we face a lot of big problems, but we can start fixing them through a lot of small actions.... If each one of you takes action, you will create a wave of action like this world has never, ever seen. Be a part of two billion acts for good. Because, step by step, little by little, we will get to a better world. Together let's get the job done."
—Amina Mohammed, UN Deputy Secretary-General

Autumn Peltier, Canada

"I think of future generations and my grandchildren and their grandchildren. Will they even have clean drinking water?"

Autumn gifts the Prime Minister with a traditional water bundle.

Autumn is from Wiikwemkoong Unceded Territory, on Manitoulin Island, Ontario. "Since I was a little girl, my aunt and my mom have been teaching me about the importance of clean drinking water." Autumn's aunt, Josephine-ba Mandamin, was called Water Walker for her walks around the Great Lakes. "She is the one who inspired me to do the work that I am doing. I advocate for water because we all came from water and water is the only reason we are here today, living on this earth. Nothing can survive without water. Water is alive and has a spirit. Water is sacred. There are many First Nations communities that cannot drink their water. Canada is one of the richest countries in the world. Why should our people be living in these conditions? When I had the chance, I told Canada's Prime Minister that I was very unhappy with the choices he has made. He said he understood. Then I started crying. When I speak to kids, I always tell them that they could do the work I am doing. I started public speaking and advocating in my own community. It just progressed from there. Everyone must help with the clean water issue, recycling, and taking care of the environment. I will not stop praying and fighting until my people have clean drinking water." On World Water Day 2018, Autumn spoke to the UN about the need for clean drinking water around the world.

Autumn says:
Anybody could do this work and if we all come together, we can hopefully make a big change.

"Oh Poop, It's Worse Than I Thought." At age 11, after learning that sewage from toilets was emptied into a nearby river, **Stella Bowles** tested the water quality for her Canadian National Science Fair project. High levels of fecal contamination prompted the government to clean up the river.

When Canadian **Marcus Deans** was 12, he was shocked to see a photo of a girl in West Africa having to drink filthy brown water and to learn that a billion people in the world do not have clean, safe drinking water. That began Marcus's mission. He invented NOGOS, a low-cost water filter using everyday materials. "One of the worst times was when I put clean water into the filter and it came out black. I wanted to give up, but I knew that if kids my age could spend hours a day getting water, I could also persevere and complete my work."

Jaelun Parkerson, USA

"We're trying to put a change in the world, but other people are scared to."

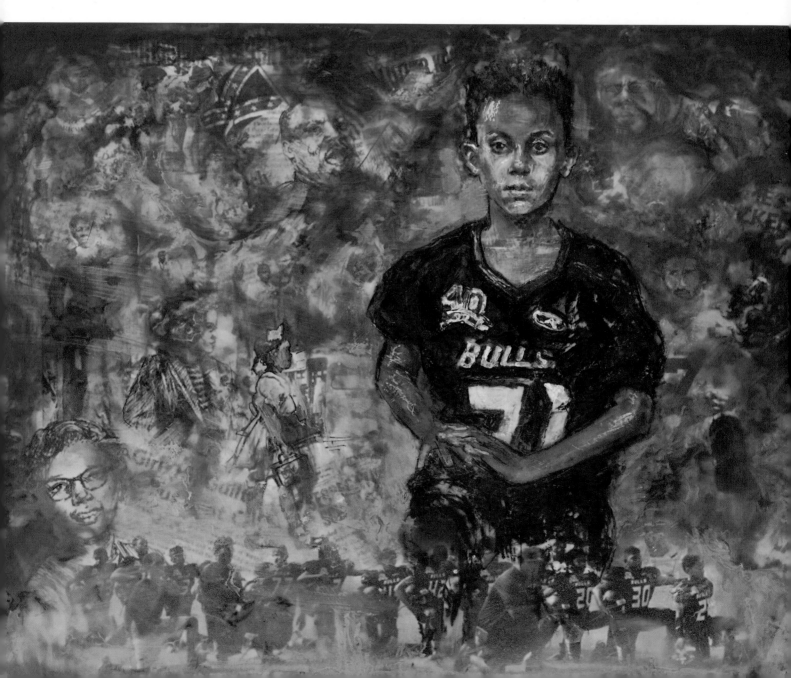

The Beaumont Bulls take a knee with Jaelun, Number 21.

In 2016, white policemen were caught on video shooting a black man in two separate incidents, sparking protests and riots in the US. Jaelun Parkerson, then 11, was shocked. "Why are black people being killed for no good reason by white police?" he asked his parents. "What can we do?" Then Jaelun saw pro football player Colin Kaepernick protesting police brutality by kneeling on the field during the national anthem, the same bold gesture taken by heroes of the civil rights struggles in the 1960s. This was what he could do! Jaelun took the idea to his football team and their coach. Rah-Rah Barber asked, "Are you boys sure you know what you're protesting?" What came back was no surprise. They all wanted to protest racial injustice and brutality. "Soon we won't be boys. We'll be black men," Jaelun said. "We don't want to worry if the color of our skin makes us a target." At the next game, each player knelt during the anthem. Many spectators were furious! Officials gave warnings, but most players repeated the action. When their coach was fired, the boys refused to play until he was reinstated. Rah-Rah said, "Our kids are waking up and when that happens, change happens." Even after forfeiting their season and receiving death threats, the boys stayed strong. Jaelun insisted, "I would have kept on taking that knee."

Jaelun says:

When people say they should lynch us and burn us, it disappoints me, because everybody is the same deep down—they just don't know it.

After the US travel ban against majority-Muslim countries, **Hebh Jamal**, 17, organized a mass student walkout in New York City to protest Islamophobia: "This ban affects thousands of immigrant students. We should be able to have a say and voice our opposition. In the civil rights movement, there were sit-ins and walkouts. Students were on the forefront of the movement. We needed to do the same, but on our terms."

"When it comes to justice, there is no easy way to get it. You have to take a stand and say, 'This is not right.' And I did." In 1955, **Claudette Colvin**, 15, was arrested and jailed for refusing to give up her bus seat to a white woman. Her court case ended bus segregation in the US state of Alabama.

Melati & Isabel Wijsen, Indonesia

"Instead of asking if the change is going to happen, we ask when it will happen."

Melati and Isabel's dream became a reality.

Melati and her sister Isabel attended The Green School, where students were encouraged to be the solution to environmental problems. "When I was 12, I had this feeling that I could not wait until I was older to start making a difference. After being inspired by a lesson about real people who had made a difference—like Nelson Mandela—my sister and I wondered, 'what can we do as kids living on Bali? What can we do now?' We could see firsthand the negative impacts of plastic pollution. It was everywhere. So, in combining our concern about plastic pollution with the inspiration from the classroom, we created a movement. It was so simple; without a business plan, a strategy, or even a budget, we started our own company called Bye-Bye Plastic Bags with our passion and our pure intentions." The sisters petitioned the government to ban plastic bags, but after two years of being ignored, they staged a hunger strike. Police threatened the girls with jail. But their protest worked! The governor signed an agreement to make Bali free of plastic bags. And Indonesia is planning the same, thanks to Melati and Isabel. "We are the first generation to live through these challenges and to experience the extreme changes in our climate up close. It is a matter of making the right decisions to keep working towards a future that we want to be a part of. We youth may only be 25 percent of the world's population but we are 100 percent of the future."

Melati says:
To all of the kids in this beautiful but challenging world—go for it! We're not telling you it's going to be easy. We are telling you it's going to be worth it.

Edgar Edmund Tarimo was 15 when he decided to do something about the mountain of plastic waste in Tanzania. He spent his birthday money to buy materials to build a plastic-converting machine. His parents didn't approve of Edgar's collecting, but three years later, his business, Green Venture Recycles, had dozens of employees and was making a profit. As Edgar notes, "People were building mud houses because they can't afford stronger clay bricks. We now have the strongest bricks and roof tiles made out of plastic that resist rain and floods."

Hannah Testa believes knowledge is power. "A plastic straw is used for about 20 minutes but it lasts forever in a landfill. Half of the 1 billion straws used worldwide come from the US." The teen activist from Georgia founded Hannah4Change to raise awareness about plastic pollution.

"I just hope kids see they don't have to hide anymore."

Jesse wants hockey to be open to everyone.

High school was not always easy or fun for Jesse. But he found a way to cope. "Hockey was an escape from what was actually going on—in school and my personal life. When I was on the ice with my team, nothing else mattered. Then the team found out that I was born a girl. Even though I identify as male, I wasn't allowed to change with my male teammates according to our minor league rules. Because I had to go into another change room, I began to feel left out. I missed team conversations and plans to hang out with my buddies after the game. But then I'd also get kicked out of the girls' change room because parents thought I was a guy. I was always in a hard place, and I just got sick of it! I didn't want people to think about me being transgender. I wanted to be Jesse the guy—just like any other teenager growing up." Jesse considered quitting hockey. "But then I realized I had to let other transgender people know that someone was standing up for them." He filed a complaint against Hockey Canada with Ontario's Human Rights Tribunal to protect his gender identity. Gender Identity is how one feels inside about being male, female, neither gender, or both. Transgender (or trans) people identify differently from the gender assigned at birth. Jesse won his case. Rules now allow trans players to use the facilities of their choice and to be referred to by their preferred name and personal pronoun (they, them, he, him, her, she). Thanks to Jesse, their trans status is now confidential.

"I believe in sharing my story about being transgender and experiencing depression and anxiety so others know they're not alone. Coming out as LGBT+ has been a positive experience," says **Kieran Drachenberg**. At 15, he helped pass a bill that protects gender identity in Nunavut, Canada. He promotes youth mental well-being by raising money and volunteering for Kids Help Phone, encouraging Indigenous Northern youth to seek help if they need it.

"I took action so that no one else would have to suffer as I did." When **Nicole Maines** was in fifth grade, she was not allowed to use the girls' washroom. She felt humiliated and experienced bullying. After suing the school, a judge in her US state (Maine) ruled it unlawful to deny transgender students access to washrooms.

Xiuhtezcatl Roske-Martinez, USA

"My generation is rewriting history by holding our leaders accountable for their disastrous and dangerous actions."

Xiuhtezcatl speaks passionately to raise awareness.

He was just a little boy when Xiuhtezcatl first realized the power of his voice. "Since I was 6, I've been on the front lines of environmental movements standing up to fight for my future and for our planet. What a lot of people fail to see or seem to ignore is that climate change isn't an issue that's far off in the future. It isn't slowly affecting the ice caps or the sea-level rise. It's affecting us right here, right now, and will only continue to get worse. Frequency and severity of wildfires, massive floods, and super storms—all are increasing because of our lack of action, because of the increase of carbon dioxide emissions, because of the way we are living. And, because of this, young people are standing up all over the planet. We see that climate change is a human rights issue. It is affecting developing countries, women, children, and people of color more than anyone else. We need to reconnect and end this mindset that we can continue to take whatever we want without giving back or understanding the harm that we are doing to the planet. Every generation is remembered for something: climate change is defining our generation. So, do we want to be remembered as the generation that destroyed Earth, or as the generation that changed our relationship with Earth?" —Excerpted from Xiuhtezcatl's 2015 speech to the UN.

Xiuhtezcatl says:

We are being called upon to use our courage, our innovation, our creativity, and our passion to bring forth a new world. I don't want adults to stand up for us. I want them to stand up with us.

Twenty-five youth took the Colombian government to court in 2018 to stop destruction in the Amazon rainforest. The mission was called impossible, but the judge sided with the young people, recommending that they be consulted on sustainable action plans to combat deforestation and reduce greenhouse gases. This victory paves the way for other global youth taking similar legal action for their human right to a stable climate system.

"You failed us. It's your responsibility to protect the youth. But when faced with the choice of fossil fuel money for your campaigns, or the well-being of your children, you pick fossil fuels." —**Jamie Margolin**, 16, USA, founder of Zero Hour

Tiassa Mutunkei, Kenya

"We will not be the generation that allows our wildlife to become extinct; we are the generation that will save it."

Tiassa visits a sanctuary for orphaned baby elephants.

Tiassa earned her nickname, Animal Girl. While the other girls were playing with dolls, she was digging up worms. "I like people," she says, "but I like wildlife more. I have always been fascinated by animals, especially elephants." But then, Tiassa discovered something she could not ignore—poachers killed elephants for their tusks. "I was so distraught. It made no sense to me. Ivory is not a need. And it's unacceptable that people come to our country to kill such beautiful creatures just so they can make decorations out of their tusks. I started a club in my school—Teens for Wildlife—to create awareness about the threat of poaching; to share thoughts and ideas about how we could protect elephants. We take pride in our wildlife because it is our heritage. Animals are Africans, too. We should honor them and use our voices to speak up for them. If we continue to lose elephants at this rate, the younger generation will be the biggest loser. But time is running out. We cannot wait for the current generation to 'give' us back our wildlife." A 2018 World Wildlife Fund report claims global wildlife populations have fallen by 60% in just over 40 years due to man-made factors. "We are the first generation to know we are destroying our planet and the last one that can do anything about it."

Tiassa says:
No matter how young you are, you have a voice. It's your biggest tool, and it will take you places.

When **Nellie Shute** was 12, an elephant tusk was displayed at her Hong Kong school. Horrified that an elephant died for that tusk, she began a campaign among her classmates to change traditional attitudes about buying ivory for decoration. These "Elephant Angels" wrote letters, collected signatures, and staged protests urging leaders to destroy stockpiles of tusks to discourage poachers, leading to the ban of the sale of ivory in Hong Kong.

New Zealander **Taylor Finderup** is helping to save sharks from extinction because of their horrific slaughter for shark-fin soup. "Like the sharks, we are intelligent, strong, and bold. We possess limitless courage and tireless passion, and, most importantly, we are all about action and bringing about change. If I alone can educate thousands of people and get them all thinking, what would an entire generation be able to do if we all came together?"

Ta'Kaiya Blaney, Canada

"Just one empowered youth is the starting mark of a revolution."

Ta'Kaiya is from Tla'amin Nation on Canada's west coast.

Ta'Kaiya uses her talents for acting, singing, and song writing to call for action to protect Mother Earth for future generations. At 11, she co-wrote "Earth Revolution." Her lyrics are: "We're Generation Now, Children of the future, Earth's Revolution./ Creation's crying out, I feel her pain, I can't walk away./ I'll do my part to fix what's broken, and give back what we've taken, to hope for the dawn of a new day./ I'm calling each and every person, join me in Earth Revolution." Ta'Kaiya performed the song at a global conference for youth involved in social and environmental justice. "It was amazing! Someone said, 'Oh, kids, they're not going to do anything.' I said, 'Hey, I'm a kid, and you're wrong! We're speaking out for those who have no voice, like the whales, the salmon. We are not afraid to use it.' I always had a dream of creating a sustainable future for my community, but it was 'when I grow up...' When I read about an oil pipeline from Alberta to British Columbia, I realized age doesn't matter. It's important for youth to be involved because it's our future that corporations and governments are putting at risk—our water, land, and the future of Indigenous people. Elders and other inspiring people are leading this movement, but they get tired. Youth can help. Each one of us has a gift. We should share it!"

Ta'Kaiya says:

Our generation does not see activism just as an obligation, but a beautiful opportunity to invent the unexpected and to spread our optimism to make a better world.

"There is a fire lit inside you, and that fire is rising in the youth. You can feel it in the ground. You can hear it in the trees. You can feel it in the air. This generation is ready."
—**Naelyn Pike**, 17, USA

A Lakota prophecy predicts children will provide leadership when people have grown ashamed of mistreating Earth. "The Seventh Generation will rise and create a new world. It's our responsibility to stand up and protect Mother Earth for the next seven generations. We are the ones we've been waiting for!"
—**Journey Zephier**, 15, USA

"Grown men can learn from very little children, for the hearts of the little children are pure. Therefore, the Great Spirit may show to them many things which older people miss."
—**Black Elk**, holy man of the Oglala Lakota Sioux

Alex Myteberi, USA

"Kindness protects life. Use the power of kindness to help everyone."

US President Obama invited Alex to visit him at the White House.

In 2016, 6-year-old Alex stared at the disturbing image on the news of a boy his own age, his face and hair clotted with blood. Alex's parents explained that the boy's home in Syria had been bombed. Alex decided to write a letter. "Dear President Obama, Remember the boy who was picked up by the ambulance in Syria? Can you please go get him and bring him to our home?...We will be waiting for you guys with flags, flowers, and balloons. We will give him a family and he will be our brother. Catherine, my little sister, will be collecting butterflies and fireflies for him. In my school, I have a friend from Syria, Omar, and I will introduce him to Omar. We can all play together. We can invite him to birthday parties and he will teach us another language. We can teach him English too.... Since he... doesn't have toys, Catherine will share her big blue stripy white bunny. And I will share my bike and I will teach him how to ride it....Thank you very much! I can't wait for you to come! Alex, 6." Fortunately, the boy Alex had seen on TV recovered and was able to stay in Syria. But the President was so proud of Alex that he read his letter at a UN Refugee Summit. "Those are the words of a 6-year-old boy...," President Obama said. "We can all learn from Alex."

Alex says:
We should look at how children feel and how hurt they are even though they are not from your country.

"No one wants to flee the home where they were born. But when I was 14 years old, war had been going on in Syria for two years. We thought at any moment we might die from one of the bombings. Things got so dangerous and it was hard to get food." When **Muzoon Almellehan** escaped the war, she brought only the possessions she most needed—her schoolbooks.
"I could not accept that war could take everything. Nothing can take away your knowledge. And as refugees we needed education more than ever to face the challenges and suffering in our lives." Muzoon advocated for children's education while in refugee camps. Later, she became UNICEF's youngest-ever goodwill ambassador.

Refugees are people who flee their country because they are in danger. An estimated 50 million children are displaced from dangerous conflict zones. Many countries allow refugees to resettle; many still do not.

Mackenzie Murphy, Canada

"Find a reason to look beyond the darkness and hold on until the light comes shining through."

Mackenzie shared her story at We Day in Alberta in 2015.

In sixth grade, Mackenzie was enveloped in a dark cloud of depression. She was experiencing bullying both in school and online. "I had typical teen struggles and an underlying mental illness, but the bullying pushed me down to the lowest point in my life. I felt like nobody cared. I truly thought that everyone would be happier if I was gone. And so, at 13 years of age, I attempted to take my life." But in that very dark place, she found the motivation to act against bullying instead of giving in to it. "My mom called me in the hospital and told me that one of my friends was getting bullied for defending me. So, I thought to myself, 'Enough is enough! I'm no longer fighting this battle for myself—I'm doing it for my entire community.' I proposed an anti-bullying bylaw that would see fines for offenders who torment others. This would assist the police, provide a safety net for victims, and give counselling support to the bullies." In 2013, Mackenzie's bylaw was passed. "I moved from a victim to a survivor by using my knowledge and power to enact change. It was so comforting to know that bullying wasn't an issue I alone faced. Since then, I have been raising awareness about the effects of bullying on mental health. It's mind-blowing to think that I went from such a dark place to sharing my story with kids who could have ended up in that dark place."

Mackenzie says:

I don't regret what I went through because it helped open my eyes to the beautiful things in the world that I didn't really look at before.

Cyberbullying uses social media to inflict emotional pain and damage reputations. The Red Cross says, **THINK** before you post. Ask yourself, is it **T**rue, **H**elpful, **I**nspiring, **N**ecessary, and **K**ind?

"Older people are uncomfortable talking about suicide because it is a touchy subject. That doesn't mean it shouldn't be touched. We have to take the first step to have these conversations using our voices and social media." After a childhood friend ended his life, **Loizza Aquino**, 15, tweeted about a mountain climb that began in pitch blackness and ended in a beautiful sunrise. "If you died at 5:10, you wouldn't be able to see the beauty at 6:00." When reactions flooded in from strangers sharing their own struggles with depression and hopelessness, Loizza started Peace of Mind Canada, a place where youth share their dark thoughts and experiences with people who listen without judging.

Ke'Shon Newman, USA

"All of us, no matter how young, want change."

Ke'Shon paints signs for a protest against gun violence in America.

The first time Ke'Shon had to run from a shootout he was just a small first-grader. He was sitting on a park bench near his school, which is in a neighborhood where it's not safe after dark. "I ducked down and ran inside my house. The gunshots were so loud." In 2016, Ke'Shon's older stepbrother, Randall, was shot and killed in a random shootout while he was walking his girlfriend to the bus stop. This is part of a speech Ke'Shon gave during the 2018 National School Walkout Day, a movement conceived by Lane Murdoch, 15, to commemorate the victims of gun violence and encourage students to write to their elected representatives to find solutions. "Randall was a loving brother and friend to all. His life mattered, just like so many others around the country. But in Chicago, the gun violence has become a tragic way of life. This shouldn't be the normal way of living. We don't have random mass shootings—we have daily shootings, which lead us to pray every day for our safety to and from school and for our neighborhood. This is why I'm here, because we must stop letting this become normal in Chicago. In this moment, the youth voice is rising across the country. Our voices are LOUD. Our voices are CLEAR. And, our voices are about to change HISTORY."

Ke'Shon says:
Whatever I can do or anybody else can do, I suggest that they do that, because a small difference can make a big impact.

"We have watched people with the power to make changes fail to do so. Kids are the only ones who have the energy to make change," says Emma González. After a mass shooting at their school in Parkland, Florida, **Emma González**, **David Hogg**, **Jaclyn Corin**, and **Matt Deitsch** helped organize the rally, March For Our Lives, to demand common sense gun laws for safer schools and communities. Hundreds of thousands participated in more than 800 marches. The four teens received the 2018 International Children's Peace Prize.

"March For Our Lives is one of the most significant youth-led mass movements in living memory…. I am in awe of these children, whose powerful message is amplified by their youthful energy and an unshakable belief that children can, no must, improve their own futures. They are true changemakers who have demonstrated most powerfully that children can move the world."
—Archbishop Desmond Tutu

Kids Take Action!

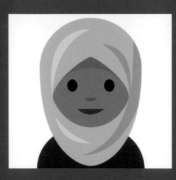

"I just wanted an emoji of me." At 15, **Rayouf Alhumedhi**, Saudi Arabia, challenged the companies who control emoji standards to create an image that represents the millions of hijabi-wearing women across the world.

"It is an outdated and silly law. And I want to throw a snowball without getting in trouble." **Dane Best** was 9 when he learned about an old law in his US hometown that banned throwing snowballs. Dane collected letters and signatures of support, researched, and presented his case to Town Council—and won! His first target was his little brother.

"I've been slapped on my face or got my hair pulled so many times at home for simply talking back to elders and expressing my opinions, only because I was a teenager. Having the right to vote is to have the right to speak." **Kim Yoon-song**, and three others had their heads shaved in front of the South Korean National Assembly to demand the voting age be lowered to at least 18.

"One in two people have menstrual periods and it's just ridiculous that we think they're embarrassing and gross. I'm on a mission to end the taboo. We have to start talking about periods without embarrassment. There needs to be much more positive education for all genders at school." When, at 17, **Amika George** discovered that girls were missing school because they could not afford sanitary products, she lobbied her UK government to provide them free to disadvantaged schoolgirls.

"Children with small actions can make big changes in the world. We only need the opportunity to do it." **José Adolfo** was 7 when he opened an eco-savings bank for kids in Peru. When children brought in recyclable items, money was deposited in their accounts. Kids became aware of consumption and the planet's limited resources, while learning how to manage money. "...my teachers thought I was crazy, but luckily, I had the support of the school principal."

"Pope Francis, I want to tell you that my heart is very sad because I'm scared that one day ICE is going to deport my parents. I have a right to live with my parents. Immigrants like my dad feed this country.... Don't forget about us—the children who suffer because they're not with their parents." When **Sophie Cruz** was 5, she learned that Pope Francis would visit the United States. She wrote a letter asking for help to save her parents from being sent back to Mexico. Sophie traveled to Washington and successfully delivered her letter. Later, the Pope asked US politicians for greater openness for immigrants and refugees.

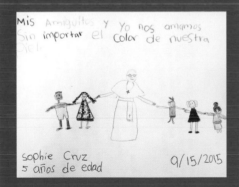

During a heat wave in the UK, teenage boys wore girls' uniform skirts to school to rebel against the "no shorts" dress code.

"Butterflies only come out of their chrysalis and fly away when the temperature is just right. I think people make a difference in the same way. When it matters most and the situation is just right, people rise to the occasion and take action." In third grade, **Genevieve Leroux**, Canada, became concerned that Monarch butterflies were endangered. She grew the milkweed plants they need during the caterpillar stage, turning her backyard into a pollinator garden. "The Butterfly Girl" raises awareness as a citizen scientist for Monarch Alert and encourages others, including the mayors of cities in Canada and the USA, to create Monarch-friendly habitats.

"Since our leaders are behaving like children, we will have to take the responsibility they should have taken long ago. So I decided to walk out of school every Friday and sit on the ground outside the Swedish Parliament to demand our politicians treat climate change for what it is: the biggest issue we have ever faced." **Greta Thunberg** was 15 when she started her protests. Since then, similar school strikes have spread around the world.

Kids Create!

"I share my story of abuse with children and encourage speaking out. If I can do it, so can they." When she was 9, **Leilua Lino**, Samoa, was molested by her father, but was too frightened and ashamed to tell anyone for years. After she told her secret to a friend, Leilua was rescued and given shelter by a Samoan support group. Leilua created a Peace Garden—a space of serenity where other violated children could heal from trauma. Leilua wants to break the silence that allows crimes against children to be committed in secret. Her presentations in schools across Samoa, have prompted many children to come forward to report abuse.

"Our time is now. Our home is here. It's not too late to save the day. Our planet needs it. Our planet needs us. It's you and I." This is the chorus of "A Better Place," written and performed by **Luca Berardi**, Kenya, one of many songs he created to spread his message for environmental action. Luca was 8 when he founded Young Animal Rescue Heroes to help protect endangered species. He shares his gifts for singing, dancing, writing, and acting to create original works that raise awareness for his causes.

An activist from age 9, **Felix Finkbeiner**, Germany, asked hundreds of the world's chocolate makers to donate 0.01% of their profits to Plant for the Planet as a "Future Fee," not one agreed. Felix was stunned. Rather than give up, his organization introduced Change Chocolate, a bar that has become the most successful fair-trade chocolate. Every purchase brings about change, from planting new trees to paying fair wages.

"I hope my paintings can give endangered animals a face so they don't disappear. And I hope I can inspire kids like me to believe they can do great things." **Bria Shay Neff**, USA, won a painting contest when she was 8. Since then she has combined her passion for art with her concern for endangered species by selling her work to raise money for non-profit organizations. Her online gallery is Faces of The Endangered.

"Why is it that the least nutritious, most sugary and food-coloring-filled breakfast cereals are marketed toward us children? Why is it that in this age of information parents are still feeding us some of the worst food on the planet, knowing good nutrition is key for proper growth and development?...You and me, the little guys grocery shopping, are the kings and queens of the land. Instead of swords or guns, we carry money. And with every purchase, we defeat the giants."
Daniel Bissonnette, Canada, has been a popular activist and social media influencer since he was 8. As a vegan, he encourages healthy eating in his book, *Daniel's Breakfast Burst*. Daniel wants kids to grow vegetables at school and home, play outside instead of playing video games, and to "get a grip on the future of our food."

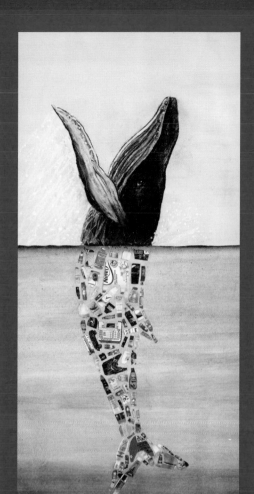

Dafne Murillo, 14, Peru—First Place Award in the Bow Seat Ocean Awareness Student Contest.

Yes, I will change, opening a new page, starting a new stage, entering a new age, in saving our world. / Because this is something we can't erase, and yet we're still choosing money over something that is irreplaceable, and here it looks alright, but over there it's disgraceful. / Because our home is dying. Our ice caps are crying. Our ecosystems are sighing, while we keep buying. / Keeping our business ships sailing, but our tips are failing to maintain our rubbish. / When did our planet deserve to be punished? —Excerpt from "We Can Be More," by **Solli Raphael**, 12, Australia's youngest slam poetry champion. (From Solli's book, *Limelight*, Penguin Random House, Australia)

What YOUth Can Do

Research. Volunteer. Persevere.

"Our advice when you begin your journey to make a difference is to follow a three-step pattern. First, research issues and find a cause you care about. Second, volunteer. Finding a local cause is best. Third, stick to that cause and put in your best efforts instead of spreading yourself too thin." Canadian twin activists, **Maryam** and **Nivaal Rehman**, used their YouTube channel, The World With MNR, to advocate for gender equality and girls' education, just like their hero, Malala Yousafzai.

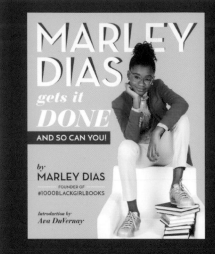

Find Your Passion

"I tell people to take their passions and blend them with activism." American **Marley Dias**'s book is a practical guide for kids who want to start campaigns. She launched the #1000BlackGirlBooks campaign to collect books with characters that looked like her.

Use Your Voice

"You should be supporting these schools, not closing them. We're going to city hall; we are not going down without a fight." The powerful speeches of **Asean Johnson**, USA, have helped save local schools from being closed in Chicago. "To prepare for a speech, I learn a lot about school closings from going to board meetings, hearings, and reading articles. I practice my speech so that I get my message out in time. I speak from my heart and say what is on my mind. Sometimes I have notes or points to help me stay on the issues. I never get nervous when speaking. Actually, I get excited and feel very powerful."

Write Letters to Important People

"I love Legos but I don't like that there are more boy people and barely any Lego girls.... All the girls did was sit at home, go to the beach, and shop, and they had no jobs, but the boys went on adventures, worked, saved people, and had jobs, even swam with sharks. I want you to go make more Lego girl people and let them go on adventures and have fun, ok!?!" **Charlotte Benjamin**, UK, was 7 when she wrote that letter that went viral. Lego listened and introduced more female characters and themes.

1-25-14

Dear Lego company:
My name is charlotte I am 7 years old and I love legos but I dont like that There are more lego boy people and barely any lego girls. today I went to a store and saw legos in two sections The pink and the blue All the girls did was sit at home, go to the beach and shop, and they had no jobs but the boys went on adventures, worked, saved people, and had jobs, even swam with sharks.. I want you to make more lego girl people and let them go on adventures and have fun ok!?! from charlotte. Thank you.

Work with an Activist Organization

"I dream of a world without child marriage, trafficking, and any form of abuse. Children will have wings, and won't be afraid of anything and are able to reach the skies." When **Anoyara Khatun**, India, was 12, she was forced to leave home to do domestic child labor. After she was rescued, Anoyara worked with Save the Children India to rescue and reunite abused children with their families. "Somewhere inside all of us is the power to change the world. Don't wait for change. Make it happen."

Use Anger as Motivation

"My anger and worry became my strength and motivation to help make our world a better place for humans, animals, and our planet. We're not just the future. We MAKE the future." At age 12, **Rachel Parent**, Canada, worried about the risks of Genetically Modified Organisms in food. She founded Kids Right To Know to get GMOs labeled on food after learning that the Canadian government was not testing the long-term effects of GMOs on our health and environment.

Organize Rallies and Lobby People with Power

"You're never too young to start making the world you want and need." Since **Rupert** (10) and **Franny** (7) **Yakelashek** learned that Canada did not have environmental rights guaranteed in the Constitution, they have worked tirelessly to persuade all three levels of government to legislate citizens' rights to clean air, healthy food, safe drinking water, and access to nature.

Acknowledgments

Thank you to all the young activists for your precious stories and wisdom that I mined for this book, and their "Dad and Momanagers" for contributing support material. Many non-profit foundations and organizations allowed me to use images freely. Their websites are listed below for readers who want to learn more about their good work or to make donations. I was fortunate to receive crucial help, guidance, and support from Marie Zimmerman. Linda Sword, Andrea Bird, and children's literature blogger Helen Kubiw gave welcome advice. Thanks, again, to the Second Story Press team. I so appreciate their willingness to tackle sensitive subjects. It was great to work with Kathryn Cole again. (She gave me my first picture book assignment more than thirty years ago.) Chris Wilson should be credited as co-producer as he worked behind the scenes so that I could be free to meet my deadlines. My love and thanks could never be enough.

I used a mixed-media encaustic technique for the illustrations. Hot beeswax, mixed with resin and oil color, is applied in layers and fused with heating tools.

The information in these thirty-two pages represents the tiny tip of the whole and ever-growing iceberg of justice issues. I recommend YouTube videos of many activists to hear moving testimonies in their own voice. I've listed helpful websites in the order the subject appears in the book.

Franny and Rupert: bluedot.ca/stories/youre-never-young-start-making-world-want/
Autumn: www.cbc.ca/news2/interactives/i-am-indigenous-2017/peltier.html
Josephine-ba Mandamin: motherearthwaterwalk.com
The Water Walker, written and illustrated by Joanne Robertson: secondstorypress.ca/kids/the-water-walker
Stella: earlgrey5.wixsite.com/stellab
Melati and Isabel: byebyeplasticbags.org greenschool.org
Hannah: hannah4change.org
Kieran: kidshelpphone.ca
Tiassa: Teens For Wildlife twitter.com/teens4wildlife wildlifedirect.org/
Xiuhtezcatl: earthguardians.org/xiuhtezcatl/ xiuhtezcatl.com
Jamie: thisiszerohour.org
Mackenzie: facebook.com/MackenzieMurphy99/ redcross.ca/how-we-help/
Loizza: peaceofmindcanada.org
Alex on YouTube: youtube.com/watch?v=F6r1kbQH8hI
Alex recommends support for refugees: Help4Refugees.org
Muzoon: unicef.org.uk/celebrity-supporters/muzoon-almellehan/

Ta'Kaiya: takaiyablaney.com
Ke'Shon: nationalschoolwalkout.net marchforourlives.com

Kids Take Action!
Rayouf: hijabemoji.org/
Dane: youtube.com/watch?v=u07pVZrlcWc
Amika: freeperiods.org
José: youtube.com/watch?v=cSfm1g3iaxl
Greta: youtube.com/watch?v=VFkQSGyeCWg
Genevieve: rootsandshoots.org

Kids Create!
Leilua: samoavictimsupport.org
Felix: plant-for-the-planet.org/en/join-in/the-change-chocolate/geschichte
Daniel: danielbissonnette.com/
Dafne: bowseat.org/programs/ocean-awareness-contest/
Solli: solliraphael.com.au

What YOUth Can Do
Maryam and Nivaal: theworldwithmnr.com
Asean: youtube.com/watch?v=oue9HIOM7xU
Marley: twitter.com/hashtag/1000blackgirlbooks
Rachel: kidsrighttoknow.com
Anoyara: savethechildren.org

Photo Credits

Franny and Rupert courtesy of Skye Ladell
#YouthvGov courtesy of Robin Loznak/ Our Children's Trust
Autumn courtesy of Assembly of First Nations
Stella courtesy of Andrea Conrad
Jaelun courtesy of April Parkerson
Hebh © Elise Blanchard
Melati and Isabel courtesy of Bye-Bye Plastic Bags
Edgar courtesy of Children's Climate Prize ccprize.org
Jesse © Nathan Denette/Canadian Press
Kieran courtesy of Ross Mingeriak
Tiassa courtesy Rosemary Muntakai
Elephant Angels © Alex Hofford
Xiuhtezcatl courtesy of Robin Loznak/ Our Children's Trust
Zero Hour March © Alex Garland
Mackenzie © Joseph Leung/We Day Alberta
Loizza © Danielle Da Silva/Winnipeg Free Press
Alex courtesy of Barack Obama Presidential Library/ Pete Souza
Muzoon courtesy of UNICEF
Ta'Kaiya courtesy of Maritza Mandinga
Journey courtesy of Robin Loznak/Our Children's Trust
Ke'Shon © John Zich/ZRimages.com

March for Our Lives courtesy of KidsRights kidsrights.org/childrenspeaceprize

Kids Take Action!
Hijab design by Aphelandra Messer
Sophie Cruz letter courtesy of her family
Greta Thunberg and José Adolfo courtesy of Children's Climate Prize
Skirts © SWNS.com

Kids Create!
Leilua courtesy of Samoa Victim Support Group
Chocolate courtesy of Plant for the Planet
Daniel courtesy of Daniel Bissonnette
Dafne art courtesy of Bow Seat Ocean Awareness Programs
Poetry excerpt from Limelight by Solli Raphael, published by Andrews McMeel

What YOUth Can Do
Maryam and Nivaal courtesy of Adam Scotti/The Office of the Prime Minister of Canada
Asean © Alex Wroblewski
Marley Dias book cover courtesy of Scholastic Inc.
Charlotte's letter courtesy of SocImages: thesocietypages.org
Franny and Rupert courtesy of Skye Ladell

Library and Archives Canada Cataloguing in Publication

Title: Our future : how kids are taking action / written and illustrated by Janet Wilson.
Names: Wilson, Janet, 1952- author, illustrator.
Identifiers: Canadiana 2019007096X | ISBN 9781772601039 (hardcover)
Subjects: LCSH: Political activists—Juvenile literature. | LCSH: Children—Political activity—
    Juvenile literature. | LCSH: Social action—Juvenile literature.
Classification: LCC HN18.3 .W55 2019 | DDC j361.2—dc23

*Second Story Press gratefully acknowledges the support of the Ontario Arts Council
and the Canada Council for the Arts for our publishing program. We acknowledge the
financial support of the Government of Canada through the Canada Book Fund.*

Printed and bound in China

Published by
Second Story Press
20 Maud Street, Suite 401
Toronto, Ontario, Canada
M5V 2M5
www.secondstorypress.ca